Pia

Positive Victory
Universal Quotations

Translations

Other languages will follow, English will remain on each page making future books bilingual.

We owe commitments
to evolve our lifestyle:
as well as positive
Perfect Planets.

Foreword

Written here over 250
positive quotations
analogies, experiences,
sayings, monologues,
maxims as reminders
to entertain and give
energy on our journey,
this book brings us in touch
with ourselves and the
rest of the World. It shows
the path to engage on
creative activities naive
and profound forever.

Pia. R. SB

Positive Pursuits   Irr-pla

I

THE PAST doesn't hold me, my
positive strength has set me free.

II

HUNGER kills people on Earth
with plentiful riches: Positive
activity can eradicate it.

III

JOY is positive activity that
makes humanity proud of.

IV

BE TRUE to yourself, metamorph
into positive love.

V

FOCUS on positive priorities
be happy; live steps ahead.

VI

BUILD productive bridges;
brake negative habits.

VII

WE OWE to imprint equality &
freedom; being positive.

VIII

ACKNOWLEDGE images of traumas
and positively move forth.

IX

LIFE change experience is a
positive turning point.

Contents

Foreword	01
Contents	03
Publishers First edition	05
Analysis	07
Index with coded alphabet	09
Acknowledgements	10
Author Background	12
Plan to translate Positive Victory into other idioms	15
First proverb-maxim	18
Storytellers, monologues up to 130	
Appendix (added 120)	87
Analogy of sketches	112
Postscript	128
Index with first line words	152
Abbreviation	162
Index last page	163

Published by: Pan2000 Publishers

First Edition produced by Panache 2000 Ltd
Date: April 2005

Second Edition August 2005
Positive Pursuits added

Author design and writing by
Pia Ross Serrano Borras©

Front Cover by D. Nasseur

© All rights reserved.
Printed on recycled paper
when available

Printed in London by Panache 2000 Ltd.
email: pan2000@btconnect.com

Analysis

Universal monologues,
proverbs, maxims are
timeless culture, human
basic values:
Philosophy for life, giving
focus to facilitate debate,
my reflections, ethics and
storytellers are in two parts
all have a vital word;
Positive, each deals with
separate individual issues.
Like fashions, they can
influence our attitudes,
as beautiful paintings,
restore our equilibrium,
to bring out our positive
energy with love.

INDEX-ALPHABET
Coded for instant recall.

	Page		Page
A1	20	N14	51
B2	24	O-15	53
C3	26	P16	56
D4	28	Q17	58
E5	37	R18	59
F6	38	S19	61
G7	40	T20	68
H8	43	U21	79
I-9	43	V22	
J10		W23	79
K11	45	X24	
L12	46	Y25	85
M13	50	Z26	

Appendix 1	87
Analogy of sketches	112
Reflections	122
Postscript	128
Reminders	151

Acknowledgements
with deepest love

To my parents:

It was my mother who
instilled in me the
value of proverbs, she
was a natural storyteller.

To my husband:

When I consulted with
him about this book,
he told me: Go for it.

Acknowledgement
with deepest love

To Dona Sara Maynair

Academic Head of the
Institute Laboral in
Alcaniz Aragon
She did relish teaching
and; Learning. 1960.

To my friend and Guru
Jane White Boswell
For many years she has
supported me, enlightening
my thirst for positive:
Knowledge.

Author Background

Born in Fornoles, Aragon Spain in 1934, Maria Pilar Serrano Borras. Parents and siblings moved to a farm, after the Civil War 1936/39. At the age of 13 and 14 i went to a Catholic school, also, I learned dressmaking, and became a professional teacher.
My school years were few but, later I took some Spanish grammar, English, and typing classes, in Alcaniz Institute Laboral.

Continued

On 1964 through Zaragoza,
Andorra and Paris, I came
to London with a working
contract. I took evening
classes, and passed exams
on textiles and drawing
at the City Guilds
Institute on May 1974.
My job was upgraded to
fashion designer and I
travelled to and fro to Paris
for inspiration. I did
retire on 1994 and started
analysing words and ideas
that I had collected for
this book. Finally, being
bilingual has encounter
a positive purposeful.

P.S Acknowledgements

I gave my special thanks to Shirin Bilimoria my friend and owner of trim decorated cat Positive Perla.

Also my special thanks to Sandra Cabral Pina who is currently translating into Portuguese, Positive Victory.

Note; There are maxims, Monologues and analogies, irregular placed, (not in alphabetical order).

Positive Pursuits   Irr-pla

IX
POSITIVE strength is
within each of us.

X
BREAK negative circles,
with positive activity.

XI
SEPARATE myths from facts,
write the truth positively.

XII
SERENITY is like one
precious diamond, beware.

XIII
REASONABLE debate must
prevail, positive persevere.

XIV
ERADICATE stigmas, with
positive attitude break free.

XV
BEWARE, our strength can
become our weakness.

XVI
SEARCH positive balance,
life is for enjoyment.

Positive Victory 17

N214 - Both Irr-pla - N215

The abyss edge is open:
But, positive
activity will hold
us back,
far-away
forever.

Do not
underline the
obvious:
Positive,
find your
strength and go forth.

Sayings = Maxims

Being positive is
essential:
Being negative is energy
& time wasted.

N 18   N18A

The key to open mysteries,
the progress path is
positive planning:
Reflecting, in control.

Positive Victory

One gram of positive
Hope, is vital:
Having one kilogram
its an achievement.

N19   N19A

Set tasks everyday, make
sure they are positive:
Innovative, accomplished,
enjoy the challenge.

All rules have
exceptions:

But, being positive
doesn't have any.

N20   N21

Adversity can be reversed
with focused activity:
Positive will power
leads to Victory.

Positive Victory

After the havoc,
peaceful time follows:
Search positive strength,
learn and move on.

N22   N23

Achievements, how to
measure them?

Looking into the eyes,
feeling positive-proud.

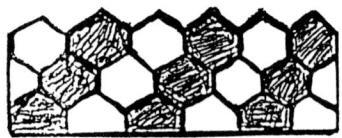

Activities reveal our aims:
Positive, lets make sure
they are our choices.

N24   N25

Acknowledge traumas, to
eliminate future ones:
Positive therapy helps,
to move forward.

Anger and envy destroys
reason, spreading havoc:
Search positive strength
to regain equilibrium.

N26   N27

All chapters in History
have several versions:
Positive, write objectively
and truthfully.

Believe in power to
change negative into;
Positive **forever**:
And you will; Triumph.

N28   N29

Be gentle like small
birds, positive and focus:
Speaking your mind, with
clarity.

Bad happenings, when
analysed, can bring
positive power:
Changing perceptions,
moving forward.

N30   N31

Break the negative cycle:
Positive, focus on issues
with universal common
principles.

Being positive, is power
without boundaries:
Endeavour, the rewards
are plenty.

N32   N33

Constructive criticism,
is positive progress:
To implement it, is vital.

Positive Victory

Compromising,
accepting to differ
is positive and noble:
Except on principles
and safety.

N34   N35

Calling help playing
fool, can backlash:
Be fair with positive
activities.

Create your everyday
turning point:
Positive, contribute to
harmony and have fun.

N36   N37

Don't let memories
or anyone take your
positive serenity:
Neither put yourself,
to their level.

Don't dwell on
suspecting:
Positive and objective,
investigate.

N38   N39

Destiny delivers heavy
crosses, painful and
mysterious:
Seek positive strength,
to move forward.

Don't dwell on guilt,
God can forgive
Instantly:
Positive, seek
forgiveness and joy.

N40   N41

Dreams we all have,
make yours unique:
Be focus use skills
and humour positively.

Don't look for
two legs on cats:
Positive,
acknowledge
facts.

N42   N43

Denial is a problem:
Acknowledge the issue,
with positive steps
eradicate it.

Beyond positive, one can
only excel and share:
Being negative, brings
only regrets:

N44A Irr-pla   N45B

Love and determination
are spices of life:
Add positive humour and
integrity to triumph.

Discipline first step,
is sorting out
priorities:
Being positive,
achievement starts.

N44   N45

Don't panic, be
positive:
On split seconds
in control, you can
choose best.

Mono of goodfeeling N46

Depression can be
fought to un end,
with positive activities.
Take a bath, and eat
your favourite food
with moderation:

Allow time for daily
toxins out of your body;
Use tablets for short time,
take some vitamins,
for a long time.
Learn to relax; Take
a holiday break:
Keep, a positive sense
of humour.

continued

Positive Victory

continued

Depression can waste valuable time; Stopping vital progress: Break the negative cycle. Move on however slow; But purposeful; Listen to music,
relax; Make a drawing; Exercise arms and legs with symmetry often.
Talk to someone; Read or write; Endlessly.
Life is for enjoyment;
But when depression persists; go for help.

Maxims

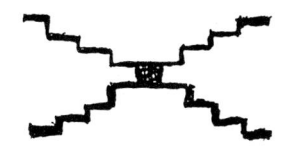

Enemies, bullies, will
attack suddenly:
Beware keep distance,
break negative cycles,
positive plan strategies.

N48   N49 Irr-pla

It's vital to see the
World like one family:
Positive contribute to
universal harmony
forever.

Everyday is a new start,
hours are like bridges:
Breathe deep, positive
with innovation.

N50   N51

Forgiving is progress,
but, don't forget:
Positive beware, unless
received, genuine;
apology.

Positive Victory

Feel positive happiness,
don't pretend:
Seek good-times,
bad-ones, arrive;
suddenly.

N52   N53

Focus on positive
activities:
Achievements come
with skills, strategies
and commitments.

Fire shapes steel:
Positive endurance
can also transform us
successfully.

N54   N55   ✡

God can forgive
Instantly; We mirror
his image:
Use your positive
intuition.

Positive Victory

Go to memory lane;
Positive, cleanse
your thoughts :
Breathe deep, plan with
discipline.

N56   N57

Groom yourself, to
succeed don't show
defeat:
positive confidence,
is power.

Genuine positive persons
express free will:
Integrity and
perseverance are their
idiosyncrasies.

N58   N59

Gratitude is a virtue,
being in love is
different:
Positive, avoid
misunderstandings.

Holding to much one
can't hold tight:
Positive, sort-out
priorities.

N60   N61

Information and
knowledge becomes
wisdom:
Positive, use it to
enlighten new enigmas.

If… and only…
feeling worried,
makes us suffer:
Be positive, might
never-happen.

N62   N63

In solitude positive
thinking brings
serenity.
In company we share
love.

Positive Victory

Identify trees by its fruits:
Positive, identify people
by their actions and
react accordingly.

N64   N65   ✡

Keep issues on their
own context:
Positive, focus
finding the truth.

Look positive through
someone else's eyes:
Gain understanding,
use it wisely.

N66   N67 Irr-pla

Resolve the cause, not
just the symptoms:
Positive, focus on
research, call the expert.

Luck is a wonderful
surprise:
Positive, endeavour to
find more opportunities.

N68	N69

Listen, feel, look
your body:
Positive react to its
needs with individuality.

Love triumphs with
actions:
Positive discipline,
flowers and humour.

N70   N71

Life is a priceless
gift, whatever length:
Be positive and happy
with commitments.

Look at issues positively
from different angles:
Plan strategies well
documented, experience
progress.

N72   N73

Learn to gain experience,
anticipate behaviors:
Positive, be steps ahead.

Mystery, angels who
went away:
Playing over the
rainbow, smiling waiting
amongst the stars.

N74   N75

My blessed money,
brings me out of
troubles:
Positive, saving ahead.

Miracles happen, focus
on positive goals:
With commitment,
skills and humour.

N76   N77

Nobody is perfect but:
Find beauty and power
on positive genuine,
activity.

At times a performance
ends, the private person
emerges:
Positive know when to emerge.

N78A   N79B   ✡

Life it's not a holiday,
it's a trial:
Find and imprint your
positive destiny.

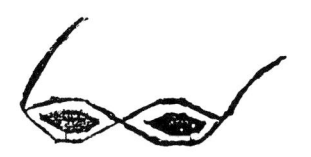

Our strength can become
our weakness:
Positive, assertive,
focus on priorities.

N78   N79

On important matters,
never make instant
decisions:
Think positive, time
alters perceptions.

Maxim-storyteller N80

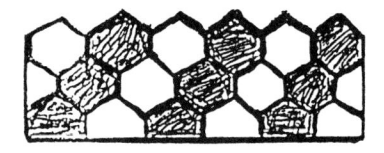

One colony of honey bees with its hexagonal cells, picking up wax and delicious honey; They are creative, discipline and productive; Throughout The Millenniums: Throughout our life we should observe, learn from other species, invaluable attributes are not, just our monopoly; Lets plan ahead, feel free happy, being part of the positive human race.

Positive and perceptive
speak with clarity:
To succeed, substance
and timing are vital.

N81   N82

Principles are humanity
pillars:
Lets acknowledge some;
Positive; Peace; Progress;
Integrity; Justice
and Love.

Punishment must be
positive and fair:
Excessive punishment,
will not help to move on.

N83   N84

Problems get bigger, if
we allow them:
With positive analysis,
eradicate them.

Positive don't give up,
what cost you dear:
Humanity needs
entrepreneurs
researchers.

N85 N86

Question your actions:
When out of order,
do something positive
to apologize.

Positive Path

Research is commitment
to solve; Positive
vital issues:
With professional,
integrity.

N87   N88

Relationships,
must have positive
mutual trust:
Accepting to differ and
every one being equal.

Freedom and responsibility
are bound together:
As long as it's positive
enjoy both.

N89A   N90B

Use knowledge, prayer and
positive perseverance
anytime to win the issue:
Afterwards thank Heaven.

Positive Victory

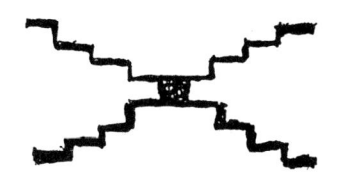

Rise above adversity,
positive, in control:
Endeavour to survive
with skills and pride.

N89   N90

Stand for your rights,
positive, helping others:
All human-beings are
equals.

Monologue

N91

See the sun, moon, rainbow colours, the oceans, fishes and birds, the Earth, trees, fruits, flowers; Breathe the perfumes and oxygen; Think positive:
See women, men, children and other creatures… Technology, sciences, living and progressing in harmony with each other; Lets contribute to make our mark with love.

Someone is jumping into
the abyss:
Be positive help to
break the cycle.

N92 ✡ N93

Stop crying, feel the
joy of living:
Pause, learn, search for
positive equilibrium
forever.

Smiles brings happiness,
laughter is wonderful:
Positive make it happen.

N94 ✡ N95

Stay positive with
serenity:
Wishing the same for
all mankind.

Statement of faith N96

See the damage caused
by thunderstorms, rivers
overflow, hurricanes
devastation, earthquakes,
lives lost; Man-made
wars; Hunger in a world
of plenty:
Bad happenings, when
analysed, can bring positive
power. Never give up on life.
Let's take positive actions.
God is testing our loyalty
and love; He is:
everywhere our positive
permanent witness.

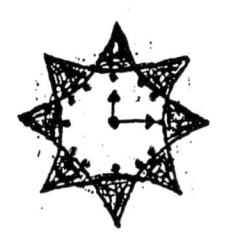

Time for healing is
needed, when emotions
are deep-felt:
Being positive is vital

N97		N98

The sound of laughter
is like a tonic:
Positive, participate and
channel to others.

Positive Victory

The greatest achievement
is to overcome adversity:
Positive recount the
story, learning from it.

N99   N100

To acknowledge ones
limitations is wise:
Positive, it has wisdom
to play for advantage.

Talk with no actions
is seldom progress:
Positive inertia is
the exception.

N101   N102

There are schools of
positive thinking:
With space for one
of your own.

Time alters perceptions,
separating trivia from
principle:
Positive learn to be
discerning.

N103   N104

There are no doors,
separating day from
night:
Positive, never give up.

Monologue - Reflections

The power of being positive
can eradicate evil:
Learn from History;
"United we stand"...
be counted, plan for a
positive Century, negotiate
pursuing peace, the
Universe is ours to share

Monologue   N105A

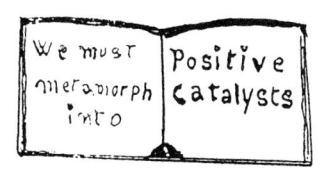

> We must metamorph into Positive Catalysts

There are rules in
books saying; You can't
do this or that, but
on the opposite page
explains how you can:
Planning ahead, being
positive with activities,
persevere and you can win

Theology is for experts,
like doctors, scientists
and other professions:
Positive, contribute
anyway possible.

N106 ☆ N106A irr-pla

Trust is always man's
best friend:
But if you lose it,
positive move forth.

Positive Victory

The choice is ours, to
put theories into use:
Positively, lets take
responsibility for it.

N107 ☆ N108

The best word is yet
unspoken:
Positive, stay focused
timing is vital for winning.

Think positive,
favourite things only:
Leave no space for
unwanted ones, focus
with perseverance.

N109   N110

Statement of Faith

There are many;
Religions, traditions,
but, only one God:
Faith, is personal,
be positive.

Positive Victory 77

The issue is not us
taking, but, us giving:
Positive and purposeful.

N111   N112

The leading path to end
conflicts is with positive
debates:
Love and loyalty helps.

The quest of positive
leaders is to bring
clarity forever:
To strategies that
triumph.

N113   N114 Irr-pla

Positive proverbs-maxims
are rewarding reading:
But, they are not
substitute for prayers.

Positive Victory

United on positive
issues is power:
Divided, achievements
are proportionate and
still vital.

N115 ✡ N116

When we share sadness,
it becomes half:
Sharing positive happiness,
they become double ones.

Wish to others, the same
as for yourself:
Positive with
commitments, have fun.

N117   N118

We behave according
to knowledge:
Positive education is
like oxygen, vital
for living.

When people can't
collect a harvest:
Positive they go
picking blackberries,
tea, flowers, etc, etc.

N119   N119A

When our positive
subconscious inspire
daily activities,
we are winning:
Creating like a genius.

One step up and down
it's not progress:
discipline & positive
planning it is.

N120 Irr-pla - both - N120A

A breakdown is madness:
Acknowledge positive
perceptions as the way
forth to sanity.

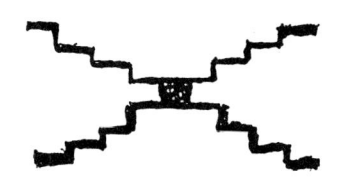

Monologue   N121

All human beings are born
free, with equal rights,
lets be positive:
To give and receive is a
two way road, contribute to
harmony, perceptive creative
with a sense of humour and
love.

We cope with hardship,
positive regain control:
Work for happy times
we deserve them.

N122   N123

We can stop negative
attitudes:
Lets look for positive
self-esteem with commitments.

You can't win all games:
Think positive, focus
to win next.

N124   N125

Your triumph is in trying,
winning is a bonus:
Be positive with
innovative strategies.

Appendix

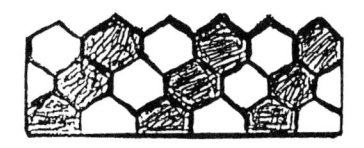

Association of ideas
brings creativity
and progress:
Make yours positive
with laughter.

N126   N127

Be positive with self-
esteem:
Give inspiration, with
integrity into best human
principles.

Before breaking positive
rules:
Think of the **forever**
consequences.

N128   N129

Don't become a villain,
after being a victim:
Positive, implement
your rights.

Appendix

Death is mystery, crying
release emotions:
Positive, find the
meaning of life.

N130   N131

Don't whistle at my
troubles: Be positive,
pass no criticism that
is derogatory.

Appendix

Ego stands on the way of progress:
Positively, eliminate egos to regain equilibrium.

N132 ✡ N133

Everyday is a free gift:
The main key to happiness is positive activity.

Appendix

Statement of faith

Eternity will rejoice
broken minds:
Positive gain merits
for the encounter.

N134 ✡ N135

End hostilities with
reasonable debate:
Positive endurance can
bring trust again.

Appendix

Knowledge and logic are
ingredients for a positive
living:
Learn to find them.

N136 Irr-pla - both - N137

Let's share the Earth,
food and cultures:
Positive with commitments
and inventiveness.

Positive Victory

△△▽△△

Envelops speak for
themselves:
But, it's the positive
lifestyle that matters.

N136A   N137B

Comment on positive
impressions:
Use adversity to advantage,
building bridges with
patience and humour.

Appendix

Vital activity is needed
to eradicate pain and
poverty:
Positive people can
Contribute substantially.

N94A Irr-pla - both -N94B

Trivial, derogatory and
vulgar are negative
cul-de-sacs:
Break bad habits with
Positive planning.

Monologue

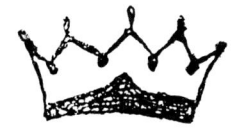

Freedom to loneliness
wake up, positive groom
yourself, regain confidence
use independence to your
advantage, cultivate
friends among equals
be one; Share hobbies with
love enjoy life.
Seek advice, when needed.

Appendix

Follow positive dreams
literally:
Find their meaning, until
you reach full circle.

N139 Irr-pla - both - N139A

Silence is an integral
part of a dialogue:
Positive, objective and
substance are forever
winners

Positive Victory

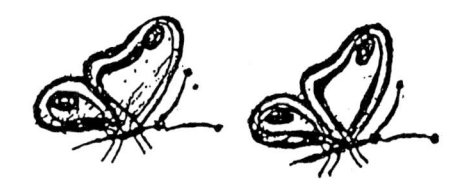

Maxim Story   N140

Look at butterflies beauty
they were vegetarians
caterpillars, producing
useful silk, before they;
Metamorphosis :

Be positive, creative,
contribute to the
universal order with ethics,
to make your mark,
persevere.

Appendix

Nothing happens, until
it has:
Positive, do your best
before, and after.

N142   N143

Nobility is being
positive, magnanimous,
trustworthy, proud and
humble:
Among equals, be one.

Appendix

Positive justice,
brings equilibrium:
Excessive punishment,
will not help to move on.

N144   N145

Pain can be reduced to
discomfort:
Positive, seek alternative
medicine or conventional.

Appendix

Reasonable debate must prevail:
To obtain positive progress, persevere,
with integrity.

N146   N147

Stigmas are prejudiced legacies:
Being positive we can eradicate such misjudgements.

Appendix

Stop trivia and
creativity will start:
Positive with skills
and commitment.

N148   N149

Search peace of mind,
find serenity:
With positive strength,
facing weakness.

Appendix

The dividing line
between love and sex
is to care:
Be positive and honest.

N150 ☆ N151

There is a rough diamond
inside us:
Positive, find it and
cultivate it.

Appendix

With positive actions,
learn to say no:
Make your turning point
loving without compromise.

N152 ✡ N153

Win over fear, with
positive planning:
Endeavour, focus and
Purposeful.

Appendix

Emotions are feelings
to be acknowledged:
Positive poetry and
psychology, helps to
move on.

N154   N155

Let's deal with problems
head-on:
Well documented positive
issues, are prescriptions
for victories.

△△▽△△

Ancestors legacies can
shape our lives:
Positive activities will
inspire present and future
generations.

N156   N157

The philosophy of being
positive is vital:
To fulfil humanities
aspirations.

Appendix

To overcome adversity is
an achievement:
Positive psychology is
one step that helps.

N158   N159

Some issues are private:
Positive, keep them under
control, secret indefinitely.

Appendix

Positive people will
give it a chance:
Or, it could be their loss.

N160   N161

Being positive is a
right turning point:
Endeavour, be focused
to reach victory.

Appendix

When in a hurry,
plan slowly:
Positive attitude,
and focus are
winning ways.

N162 ☆ N163

Beware of behaving like
a lion, shark, or
 foolhardy:
Positive, metamorphosis
yourself, into love.

Appendix

Integrity, fidelity, loyalty,
are moral values:
Positive, endeavour on
the journey to Victory.

N164 ✡ N165

There is a human being
in each of us:
Let's accept positive
Universal challenges.

Maxim Story   N166 Irr-pla

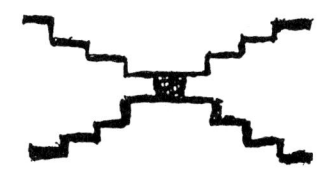

The road to perfection
is long but, never give up,
plan ahead with detail:
Let's walk on the positive
path ; Researchers on
statistics will show, at
the end Victory.

Analogy   N167

P. King
Rambo

P. Perla

Sketches help to break
the monotony of writings,
with related grace, like
cats do very swiftly:
Positive pictures brings
dreams into reality,
lifting the spirit of
wonders like maxims do.

The Mind's Windmill　　N168

Symbols have life in
their own silence:
They remind us of
material
and abstracts,
traditional
believes
and cultures.

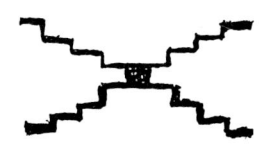

Diagonal Steps

The Cross Circle　　　　　　N169

Designs can enhance positive words, adding substance, with parallel meaning of their own: Drawings are reminders without words; Don't be too graphic, sharks bite hard. "Beware"

The Progress Bridge

Star Wonder N170

Life is about balance and fairness: Positive words with illustrations are to complement each other, showing style, vision and wonders.

The Scales

Star Clock Analogy N171

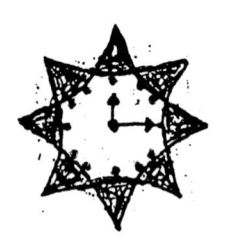

The blending of positive
illustrations with maxims
stories, is like the art of
photography:
When well arranged,
it could stand the test
of time.

The Crown

Positive Path N172

The flowers and fruits
of each season are a
wonder:
Nature has a beauty
of its own, it is our
responsibility to be
positive loving keepers;
Drawings are reminders.

Rose, Carnation & Thistle

Analogy Diamonds   N173

Pia's logo

Two diamonds overlapping
represent for me the positive
human body & the spirit.
The colour of crystals
can influence our moods,
towards positive activites.

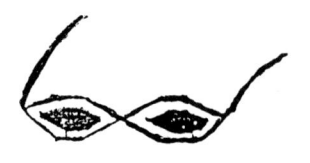

Sun glasses - crystals

Butterflies Analogy   N174

Drawings are like mirrors
acting as catalyst for our
positive aims, to become
real: Writings are tools
to help the metamorphosis.

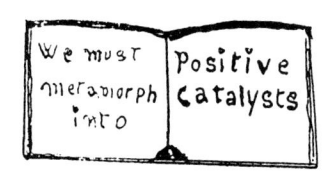

The Knowledge Book

Enigmatic triangle N175

△▲▽△△

Triangles in a pyramidal
upside-down shape, have
a double meaning:
Positive diagrams are
powerful reminders of
past and present traditions.

Sand Clock

Oil lamp

N176

Let's make the right turning point, when the light of the imagination is in a positive focus: With amalgamated symbols and universal monologues.

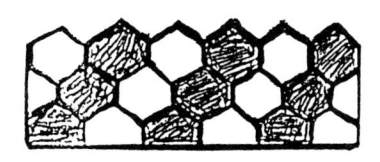

Honeycomb

Reflections

Don't lock your feelings,
seek self-esteem with
commitments:
Positive challenge can
bring hope

N177   N178

Deal always with issues
which confront you:
Positive, endeavour to
reach full circle.

Reflections

History repeats itself,
lets be steps ahead:
Break negative circles,
positive with innovations

N179   N180

Truth and freedom, they
are not commodities:
Lets respect them, feeling
proud behaving positively

Reflections

Keep promises, for
yourself included:
But, changing one's mind
is wise, when positive felt.

N181   N182

Let's search positive
justice with wisdom:
Breath deep, contribute
to universal freedom.

We owe progress to
mankind achievements:
Let's follow our quest,
positively with innovative
strategies

N183   N184

Positive debate, is the
key issue:
This is the tip, planting
seeds of Victory.

Monologue Reflections N185

All things that are good,
they are in moderation,
monitor progress with
positive activity:
Experience is invaluable
asset that professionals
treasure and non-pro
benefit also.

Reflections Maxims

Fear nothing or anyone,
just move forward:
Positive, focus on
creative universal
commitments.

N185A   N186

Positive, perceptive and
patience are tools:
That lead us to
goal's Victory.

Postscript Maxims

All happenings are a test
of endurance:
Positive, seek challenges
to experience progress.

N187   N188

Be positive, stay focused:
Is the way we do things,
that counts forever.

Positive Victory

Beware, not to be
encircled on negative moods:
With positive attitude
break free.

N189   N190

Doing right constantly, we
will achieve full circle:
Positive, feel humble, proud
and happy.

Postscript

Death is a mystery,
a new beginning, not
the end:
Imprint a positive
Legacy.

N191   N192

Follow the positive path
be counted:
History is about the one's
who dare.

Postscript

Let's make a positive difference:
Helping to create something good on this Planet.

N193   N194

Let's transform hate into tolerance with positive debates:
Putting matters into context, moving forward.

Postscript

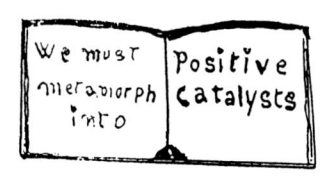

> We must metamorph into Positive catalysts

Let's fulfill our dreams.
always positive:
Cultivating mankind values
with integrity and love.

N195   N196

Storytellers will nourish
our minds:
Positive with innovations
imprinting our culture.

Postscript

Smoke comes from fire,
jealousy shows love:
Keep control, exercise
positive trust with love.

N197   N198

There are breathtaking
fashions and inventions:
But, it's the positive
message that matters.

We must use psychological language:
Reasonable debates are positive, progressive and precious like oxygen.

N198A   N199

We are philosophers pursuing knowledge:
Let's research planting positive seeds, like down-to-earth rising stars.

Monologue

N200

We owe to ourselves to
do our best at the end
of each night and day:
Positive and united
to cultivate humanity
principles is our Quest.
To win lets be focused
endeavour with skills
breathe deep and enjoy.

Analogy - Opposites   N201

Visualize with positive attitude the opposites:
- Peace and havoc;
- Freedom and fear;
- Truth and lies;
- Trust and betrayal;
- Moderation and excesses;
- Health and sickness;
- Kisses and torture:

Be focused, tolerant seek equilibrium with a creative vision learn to win.

Monologue

N202

Peace is regained when the
cycle of havoc is broken,
learning from common pain
we choose new beginnings:
Positive reasonable debate
is paramount for an ever-
lasting universal victory.

Monologue N203

Investigate fear until
there is no more; Do
nothing wrong and there
will be no fear:
Seek activities that brings
positive progress and the
precious joy of Freedom.

Monologue N204

The Truth is vital as in oxygen is for sustaining life, Integrity shines like light to expose lies: Being positive is an essential breath of fresh air.

Monologue

N205

Trust is the base of
a good relationship, but
if adversity confronts us
lets seek positive
strength learning to
move forth to find
our full Circle.

Monologue N206

Moderation can control excesses with creative strategies:
Lets be steps ahead feel issues deeper, positive endeavour to the wining line and beyond; Enjoy sharing your success.

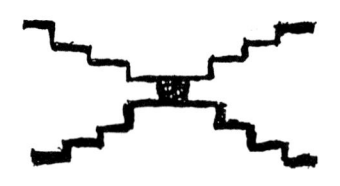

Monologue   N207

To eradicate illness focus
on research, alternative
medicine will help:
Be open minded positive
evolve, it's worth it when
in the balance is our
physical or otherwise
Health.

Positive Pursuits   Irr-pla

XVII
WIN positive records,
share & feel proud.

XVIII
ANGER & fear breaks reason,
positive regain control.

XIX
FEEL positive emotions,
find human understanding.

XX
POSITIVE & perceptive exercise humility sometimes.

XXI
METAMORPH into positive
catalyst, enjoy progress.

XXII
CONTROL your positive head,
innovative go forth.

XXIII
THE VICTORY ring shows
positive forever.

XXIV
THE SUN rise everyday
God's gift, everyone counts.

Monologue

N208

Torture physical or psychological are not acceptable in a positive fair society:
Kisses and kindness are universal expressions of friendship and love;
Beware don't live in denial.

P. King
Rambo

Maxim story Metaphor   N209

Lets make things happen,
on the journey we will
encounter choices, with
the right ones we can
shape our destiny:
Beware let no one take
our serenity, we must
metamorph into positive

continued

continued

catalysts; try to understand
others like ourselves, if
one falls regain control,
help, learn and go forth.
Positive practice leads to
Peace and Perfection.

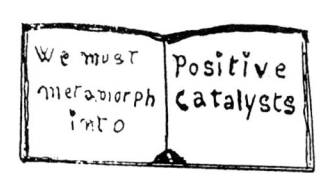

> We must metamorph into Positive catalysts

Monologue of progress N210

We must build productive
Bridges for understanding,
helping to brake negative
habits:
Creating humanity path
to share progress, from
research and the games
leading to universal Victory;
To make a difference
Everyone counts forever.

Mono's of strength

Be the positive master, open
new chapters, research and
enjoy:
Overcome adversity the
sun rises everyday God's gift;
do contribute with humour.
Beware, the strength to win
is within each of us aiming
to be better persons.

N211   N212

After seeing the edge of the
abyss, positive activity is
rewarding and vital:
Principles are still there
even when we fail; lets set
new records to feel proud;
commitments, strategies and
love are the path to Victory.

Maxim Allegory

N213

Lets love our precious
Universe, evolve and
share keeping Peace:

Love you, I love you too,
magic words when mankind
listens and responds with
positive clear echo.

▲

Pia's motto is: Positive
activity leads to Victory

Reminders

POSITIVE people can be
beaten, disappointed but,
far from finished.

▲ N216

LOOK at issues from a positive
angle to suceed.

▲ N217

TURN adversity to productive
positive advantage.

▲ N218

WHEN life gets heavy, ask
positive professional help.

▲ N219

DISCIPLINE first step,
seek positive priorities.

▲ N220

FIND and imprint your
positive destiny.

▲ N221

ENJOY, positive humour.

▲ N222

BEING positive is vital.

N223

WR words-related N.s	Page
Being positive is..... Ins-Eng-per WR N128	18
The key to open mysteries, Ins-my O WR N200	18
One gramme of positive..... Ins-my O WR N32	19
Set tasks everyday, make.. Ins-TV-Cul WR N23	19
All rules have.... Ins-my O WR N165	20
Adversity can be reversed... Ins-my MUM WR N72	20
After the havoc,..... Ins-my Mum WR N73	21
Achievements, how to.... Ins-my O WR N53	21
Activities reveal our aim: Ins-Brit-Cul WR N107	22
Acknowledge traumas, to Ins-Eng-per WR N30	22
Anger and envy destroys... Ins-Ind-Cul WR N56	23
All chapters in History... Ins-my O WR N65	23
Believe in the power to Ins-Spa-Cul WR N32	24
Be gentle like... Ins-The Bibl WR N79B	24
Bad happenings, when.... Ins-my Mun WR N45	25
Break the negative cycle: Ins-my O SWR N82	25
Being positive, is power Ins-my O WR N68	26
Constructive Criticism.... Ins-my O WR N44	26
Compromising, ... Ins-Austra-Lit WR N143	27

Index with first line

Calling help playing..	27
Ins-my Mum WR N31	
Create your everyday...	28
Ins-my O WR N76	
Son't let memories...	28
Ins-Scott-per WR N122	
Don't dwell one....	29
Ins-my O WR N84	
Destiny delivers heavy...	29
Ins-Spa-per WR N134	
Don't dwell on guilt, ...	30
Ins-The Bibl QR N51	
Dreams we all have....	30
Ins-my O WR N36	
Don't look for.....	31
Ins-my Mum WR N43	
Denial is a problem...	31
Ins-Can-per WR N84	
Beyond positive, one can	32
Ins-my O WR N53	
Love and detrmination	32
Ins-my O WR N119A	
Discipline first step, ...	33
Ins-my O WR N69	
Don't panic: be.....	33
Ins-Eng-per WR N154	
Depression can be....	34
Ins-Can-per WR N52 & N69	
Enemies, bullies, will...	37
Ins-my O WR N118	
It's vital to see the...	37
Ins-Eng-TV WR N166	
Everyday is a new start,	38
Ins-my O WR N76	
Forgiving is progress, ..	38
Ins-my O WR N40	
Feel positive happiness,	39
Ins-Spa-per WR N58	
Focus on positive...	39
Ins-my O WR N133	

Dire shapes steel.... Ins-Eng-Lt WR N36	40
God can forgive.... Ins-The Bibl WR N110	40
Go to memory lane..... Ins-my O WR N32	41
Groom yourself, to .... Ins-Spa-Lt WR N115	41
Genuine positive persons Ins-my O WR N80	42
Gratitude is a virtue Ins-my O WR N64	42
Holding to much one .... Ins-my Mun WR N107	43
Information and.... Ins-my O WR N113	43
If... and only... Ins-Can-per WR N109	44
In solitude positive Ins-my O WR N116	44
Identify tres by its ... Ins-The Bibl WR N91	45
Keep issues on their.... Insmy O WR N27	45
Look positive through.... Ins-Eng-Cul WR N73	46
Resolve the cause, not.. Ins-my O WR N87	46
Luck is a wonderful.. Ins-my O WR N36	47
Listen, feel, look.... Ins-Eng-per WR N133	47
Love triumphs with... Ins-my O WR N88	48
Life is a priceless.... Ins-my O WR N157	48
Look at issues positively Ins-Eng-Cul WR N96	49
Learn to gain experience, Ins-my O WR N118	49

Index with first line

Mystery, angels who.... Ins-Scott-per WR N142	50
My blessed money... Ins-my Mum WR N80	50
Miracles happen, focus Ins-my O WR N68	51
Nobody is perfect but: Ins-Eng-per WR N58	51
At times a performance... Ins-Scott-per WR N100	52
Life it's not a holiday.. Ins-The Bibl WR N140	52
Our strength can become... Ins-Eng-Cul WR N149	53
On important matters.... Ins-my O WR N65	53
One colon7 of honey bees Ins-my O WR 196	55
Positive and perceptive.. Ins-my O WR N113	56
Principles are humanity... Ins-my O WR N157	56
PUNISHMENT must be.... Ins-my O WR N144	57
Problems get bigger, if.. Ins-USA-Cine WR N87	57
Positive don't give up... Ins-Spa-per WR N89	58
Question your actions... Ins-my O WR N43	58
Research is commitment.. Ins-my O WR N96	59
Relationships........ Ins-Spa-Cul WR N160	59
Freedom and responsibility Ins-my O WR N195	60
Use knowledge, prayer and Ins-my O WR N136	60
Rise above adversity..... Ins-TV-News WR N21	61

Stand for yours rights.... Ins-Ando-per WR N121	61
See the sun, moon..... Ins-my O WR N157	63
Someone is jumping into.. Ins-Eng-Cul WR N45	64
Stop crying, feel the... Ins-my O WR N154	64
Smiles bring happiness..... Ins-my Mum WR N36	65
Stay positive with.... Ins-Spa-per WR N37	65
See the damage caused.... Ins-my O WR N67	67
Time for healing is.... Ins-my O WR N103	68
The sound of laughter Ins-my O WR N94	68
The greatest achievement Ins-my O WR N19	69
To acknowledge ones.... Ins-my O WR N124	69
Talk with no actions... Ins-my O WR N20	70
There are schools of... Ins-my O WR N58	70
Time alters perceptions Ins-Can-per WR N31	71
There are no doors.... Ins-my Mum WR N41	71
The power of being positive Ins-my O WR N115 & N213	72
There are rules in...... Ins-Spa-per WR N66	73
Theology is for experts Ins-my O WR N121	74
Trust is always man's.... Ins-Scott-per WR N88	74
The choice is ours, to Ins-my O WR N65	75

Index with first line

THE best word is yet.... Ins-Spa-Cul WR N72	75
Think positive ...... Ins-Cine WR N52	76
There are many....... Ins-The Bibl WR N90B	76
The issue is not us.... Ins-USA-per WR N91	77
The leading path to end Ins-my O WR N96	77
The quest of positive Ins-Eng-=per WR N72	78
Positive proverbs-maxims Ins-my O WR N42	78
United on being positive... Ins-Eng-Cul WR N28	79
When we share sadness... Ins-my Mum WR N122	79
Wish to others, the same Ins-my Mum WR N121	80
We behave according... Ins-Eng-per WR N61	80
When people can't..... Ins-my Mum WR N100	81
When the positive.... Ins-Scott-per WR N156	81
One step up and down.. Ins-my O WR N120A	82
A breakdown is madness..... Ins-my O WR N142	82
All human beings are born Ins-my Mum WR N90	83
We cope with hardship Ins-Spa-per WR N50	84
We can't stop negative Ins-my O WR N57	84
You can't win all.... Ins-Eng-per WR N20	85
Your triumph is in trying Ins-Can-per WR N190	85

Index with first line

Association of ideas.......	87
Ins-Eng-per WR N85	
Be positive with self-..	87
Ins-My O WR N186	
Before breaking positive	88
Ins-my O WR N35	
Don't become a villain..	88
Ins-Scott-per WR N31	
Death is a mystery....	89
Ins-Spa-per WR N39	
Don't whistle at my....	89
Ins-my O WR N33	
Ego stands on the way of	90
Ins-my O WR N148	
Everyday is a free gift	90
Ins-my O WR 157	
Eternity will rejoice	91
Ins-my O WR N191	
End Hostilities with..	91
Ins-my O WR N186	
Knowledge and logic are	92
Ins-my O WR N68	
Let's share the earth....	92
INs-my O WR N179	
Envelops speak for....	93
Ins-my Mum WR 180	
Comment on positive...	93
Ins-my O WR N18	
Vital activity is needed	94
Ins-my O WR N166	
Trivial, derrogatory and	94
Ins-my O WR N194	
Freedom to loneliness....	95
Ins-BBC-pro WR N105A	
Follow positive dreams...	96
Ins-Can-per WR N151	
Silence is an integral....	96
Ins-my O WR N198A	
Look at butterflies beauty	97
Ins-my O WR N209	

Index with first line

Nothing happens, until Ins-my O WR N190	98
Nobility is being..... Ins-Scott-per WR N164	98
Positive justice...... Ins-my O WR N201	99
Pain can be reduced to Ins-my O WR N207	99
Reasonable debate must Ins-Ind-Prof WR N198A	100
Stigmas are prejudiced... Ins-my O WR N161	100
Stop trivia and..... Ins-Eng-per WR N50	101
Search peace of mind... Ins-my O WR N43	101
Search peace of mind... Ins-my O WR N43	101
The dividing line.... Ins-my O WR N59	102
There is a rough diamond... Ins-Spanish-per WR N41	102
With positive actions... Ins-my O WR N34	103
Win over fear with.... Ins-Eng-Lit WR N203	103
Emotions are feelings..... Ins-my O WR N97	104
Lets deal with problems Ins-Eng-per WR N44A	104
Ancestors Legacies can.... Ins-my O WR N188	105
Ther Philosophy of being... Ins-my O WR N121	105
To overcome adversity is Ins-my OWR N198A	106
Some issues are private Ins-my O WR N90	106
Positive people will.... Ins-Eng-per WR N125	107

Being positive is a...		107
Ins-my O WR N184		
When in a hurry....		108
Ins-my Mum WR N44A		
Beware of behaving like....		108
Ins-my O WR N86		
Fidelity, loyalty....		109
Ins-Eng-per WR N180		
There is a human-being....		109
Ins-my O WR N90		
The road to Perfection..		111
Ins-my O WR N184		
Sketches help to brea....	A	112
Ins-my O WR N42		
Symbols have life in....	A	113
Ins-my O WR N185		
Designs can enhance....	A	114
Ins-my O WR N110		
Life is about balance....	A	115
Ins-my O WR N50		
The blending of positive	A	116
Ins-my O WR N103		
The flowers and fruits....	A	117
Ins-my O WR N201		
Two diamonds overlapping	A	118
INS-MY O WR N66		
Drawings are like mirrors...A		119
Ins-my O WR N140		
Triangles in a pyramidal	A	120
Ins-my O WR N28		
Lets make the right....	A	121
Ins-my O WR N190		
Don't lock yours feelings....		122
Ins-BBC-pro WR N45B		
Deal always with issues....		122
Ins-Can-per WR N44		
History repeats itself....		123
Ins-my O WR N73		
Truth and freedom....		123
Ins-Cine WR N89A		

Index with first line

Keep promises, for.... 124
Ins-my O WR N100
Lets search positive.... 124
Ins-my O WR N83
We owe progress to.... 125
Ins-my O WR N113
Positive debate, is the.... 125
Ins-my O WR N194
All things that are good.... 126
Ins-my O WR N206
Fear nothing or anyone,... 127
Ins-Eng-Lit WR N203
Positive, perceptive and.... 127
Ins-Eng-per WR N25
All happenings are a test.... 128
Ins-my O WR N193
Be Positive, stay focused.... 128
Ins-my O WR N194
Beware, not to be.... 129
Ins-my O WR N198
Doing right constantly.... 129
Ins-my Father WR N137B
Death is a mystery,.... 130
Ins-Scott-per WR N39
Follow the positive path.... 130
Ins-my O WR N166
Lets make a positive.... 131
Ins-Cine WR N209
Lets transform hate into.... 131
Ins-my O WR N31
Lets fulfill our dreams,.... 132
Ins-my O WR N115
Storytellers will nourish.... 132
Ins-my O WR N183
Smoke comes from fire.... 133
Ins-Spa-Lit WR N88
There are breathtaking.... 133
Ins-my O WR N79B

Abbreviations for Index

Austral	Australia	P	Page
Ando	Andorra	Per	Person
Bibl	Bible	Pla	Placed
Brit	British	Prof	Professor
Can	Canada	Port	Portuguese
Cine	Cinema	Rel	Related
Cul	Culture	Rep	Report
Eng	English	Ref	Reference
Ir	Irish	Scott	Scottish
Ind	India	Spa	Spanish
Ins	Inspiration	T.V	Television
Irr	Irregular	USA	United States of America
Mum	Mother	My	Myself
News	Newspaper	WR	Words related
N	Number	O.	Own
&	and	Inter	Internet
Mono	Monologue		

Note: Irregular placed Irr-pla
Not alphabetical listing

We must use psychological...	134
Ins- my 0 WR NN102 N105	
We are philosophers...	134
Ins- my 0 WR N79B & N192	
We owe to ourselves to ...	135
Ins-Eng-per WR N71 & N133	
Visualize with positive...	137
Ins-Paintings-per WR N36	
Peace is regained when...	138
Ins-my 0 WR N31 & N82	
Investigate fear until...	139
Ins-my 0 WR N153 & N138	
The Truth is vital as...	140
Ins-my 0 WR N94B & N58	
Trust is the base of...	141
Ins-my 0 WR N88 & N49	
Moderation can control...	142
Ins-my 0 WR N43 & N50	
To eradicate illness focus...	143
Ins-my 0 WR N69 & N67	
Torture physical or...	145
Ins-my 0 WR N40 & N84	
Lets make things happen...	146
Ins-my 0 WR N80 & N140	
We must build productive...	148
Ins-Inter WR N137B & N183	
Be the positive master,...	149
After seeing the edge...	149
Lets love our precious...	150
Ins-my 0 WR N209	
Pia's motto is: 011 page...	150
N214 & N215 on page 17	
Pia's philosophy on good living is lets be Positive.	163

Pia's philosophy on good living is: Lets be Positive

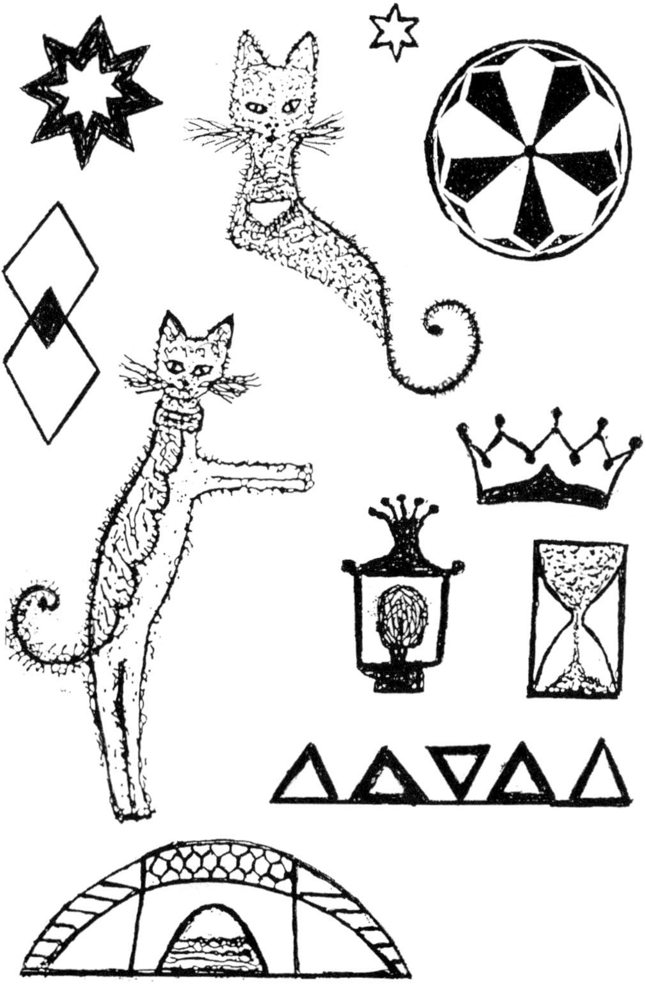